MW01138910

See the Light

Poems by

Zahara Carmi

BLACKBIRD BOOKS
NEW YORK • LOS ANGELES

A Blackbird Original, December 2022

Manufactured in the United States of America.

Cataloging-in-Publication Data

Carmi, Zahara.
See the light / Zahara Carmi.
p. cm.
I. Title.
PS3603.A75379 S44 2022 811'.6 2022949668

Blackbird Books
www.bbirdbooks.com
email us at editor@bbirdbooks.com

ISBN 978-1-61053-052-1

First Edition

See the Light

Table of Contents

One

Shine Bright..3

Summer...4

Autumn...5

The Candy Store 6

Blue...7

Rose...8

Up in the skies..9

Night...10

Icy Winter 11

Mystical Magic..12

Colors..13

Flow..14

Autumn Animals......................................15

Lovely Love..16

DNA..17

Down by the Sea......................................18

A Home..19

Flavors...20

Two

Invisible Ink..23

Writing prompts.................................24

Rainbear...25

Friendship Cake..............................26

Music to my Ears............................27

Time Machine (for the slower readers)........28

I Forgot..29

Face..30

Numbers...31

Monster in my Closet.....................32

Message in a Bottle........................33

Three

Dreams...37

Winter frost 38

Dusk Dancers..................................39

Walking in the Moonlight..............40

Thunder..41

Way Up High..................................42

Love Never Leaves..........................43

Volumes..44

Discover..45

A New Beginning............................46

Books..47

Four

If the world were made out of books..........51

Firelight..52

Clouds..53

My Name..54

Fiery..55

Keep Running...56

Five

Best Friends..59

Angel vs Devil..60

Fire, Flame, Smoke, and Stars...................61

Traveler's Song.......................................62

Still they fall..63

See the Light..64

Acknowledgements

One

Shine Bright

You will see me shine
See me shine 'cause I'm divine
And you will shine too

We will rise to the top
The top of a tall mountain
And swim through deep seas

I won't be unknown
Not to you, not to anyone
'Cause I will shine bright

Summer

Summertime is here
Let's give out a great big cheer!
Flip flops and tank tops

Sky full of sun rays
They brighten up those dark days
Sweet melon to eat!

Autumn

Leaves changing colors
The autumn is coming soon
Orange, yellow, red

Corn, squash, and acorns
Warm sweaters and leather boots
The wonderful fall

The Candy Store

Eat delicious chocolate
Yummy lollipops to lick
Delightful taffy

Strawberry pastries
Maybe have some key lime pie
You know you want to

Blue

Betwixt and Between
Unique as the sun itself
Primary Color

Not purple or green
Nor red, orange, or yellow
Gem of the rainbow

Rose

Blooming here and there
Little roses everywhere
A beautiful sight

Singing blooming rose
Dancing in the morning dew
Waiting just for you!

Up in the skies

Fluff clouds in the sky
The birds fly so very high
The sun is shining

Night

Wind howls through the night
And the majestic moon shines
A new day awaits

Icy Winter

The winter has come
And the rivers are pure slush
Snowflakes spiral down

Mystical Magic

Dragons stretch their wings
Mermaids swim through deep blue seas
Fairies fly so high

Colors

Red, orange, yellow
Greenish, bluish, purplish
Colors of the world

Flow

Water flows smoothly
If only the world could flow
With kindness and peace

Autumn Animals

Ducklings are waddling
Squirrels leaping off the trees
Wildlife everywhere

Lovely Love

Heaps of love pile up
Lovely kisses and warm hugs
There is lots of love

DNA

Fine Material
Woven very carefully
Perfect DNA

Down by the Sea

The air smells salty
Water splashes in my face
Sand between my toes

A Home

Mold coating the oak
Vines creeping through the windows
This abandoned house

Floorboards so creaky
Bluebird's chirping fills the air
A home for wild ones

Flavors

Tart, sweet, and spicy
A symphony of flavors
Playing a jazz song

Earthy, creamy, burnt
Good and bad mixed together
Shouldn't go, but they do

This food is for you
This tart, sweet, and spicy mix
This one is for you

Two

Invisible Ink

No one will see this
No one will read
I'm writing in invisible ink!
I can write something as ridiculous as I want
Or as unridiculous as I want
Doesn't even matter that that's not a word
Because I'm writing in invisible ink
How about a poem about a hippopotamus
With chicken feet that somehow
Manages to stay upright
Or a snail with shark fins that hitchhikes on kites
What is that you say?
You can see what I write?
Dang, that cheap on-sale magic!

Writing prompts

I'm having a lack of writing prompts
You see
The queen of writer's block
Would definitely be me
They say write a sonnet
About your favorite kind of tea
Thing is, I don't drink tea!
They say write a haiku
About the time you won a sports game
Thing is, I'm not a sports kid!
They say write an ode to your pet
Thing is, I haven't got one yet!
They say write a triolet
About your first holiday
Thing is, I don't remember it.
Sigh . . .
Maybe I'll just wait for it to come to me

Rainbear

While all the bears are hiding from the storm
Rainbear hops around and performs
He leaps
He spins
He twirls
He jumps
Then he swims in puddles in his trunks
Rainbear starts tapping his foot
When the storm starts brewing
And doesn't stop dancing till it does
Rainbear, Rainbear
Dance on.

Friendship Cake

First add some conversations
You can never have too much
Then a pinch of arguments
Not a lot, just a touch
Then mix in some hobbies you share
Then some spices to add flavor
Gratitude and honesty are a great pair
Then throw in some good memories
And mix it all up
Bake for 5 months, 6 months, 7 or 8
Even two years isn't too long to wait!
And there you have it, Friendship Cake

Music to my Ears

Hard Rock
Hip Hop
All the music that can make you drop
Let's have some more Reggae
Try some Classical to play
Just follow the beat
Till you find yourself cruising into Jazz
Sliding into Opera with pizzazz
Follow your own melody
Until you're ready
To share it with the world
And me

Time Machine (for the slower readers)

I have discovered the secret to time travel
Said good ol' Charlie
Oh yes, she shouted it with glee
I have a made a time machine
I needed trinkets, gadgets, parts galore
And I needed a power source even more
I found all those things easily
So now it's time for you to see
Check the time on that watch of yours
Yes this will work! I'm sure, I'm sure!
Just got to press that button
Switch that lever
Bang that drum
I'd plug my ears if I were clever
Now little boy
Check your watch again
We must have traveled at least a minute
Right?!

I Forgot

I forgot!
I forgot!
How could I forget?!
I forgot!
I forgot!
I just cannot
I don't remember where I left it last
I really need to get it fast
What did I forget, you say?
Oh, that's the thing I forgot
What I forgot
Don't look at me like that
Yes, I know I forgot *something*
Ever heard of a hunch?

Face

When I'm happy, I smile
When I'm sad, I pout for a while
When I'm mad, my jaw clenches
When I'm hungry, my chin gets drenched
When I'm surprised, my jaw drops
When I'm scared, all the rest suddenly stops
Everybody says I wear my heart on my sleeve
But I think I wear it on my face!

Numbers

One is for me
Two is for me and you
Three is for the characters in most movies
Four is for the letters in the word blue
Five is a pentagon
Six is a hexagon
Seven is for a big full week
And eight is for—
Er . . .
Eight is for . . .
You'll have to wait!

Monster in my Closet

There's a monster in my closet
I tell you, yes I do
It seeps poison into my bathroom faucet
And it leaves trails of goo
It has shaggy red fur
And big brown horns
Oh, you should hear it purr
It has crazy purple eyes
And lures kids to their demise
It says they're safe, but it always lies
And that's the monster in my closet

Message in a Bottle

A Message in a bottle
Set adrift in the sea
A message in a bottle
Found its way to me
I was digging in the sand
And guess what happened
A wave came on
And delivered a bottle to me
I took off the cap
Stuck my hand through the gap
And I found this paper
My mom said it was a caper
But I didn't think so
So I said no
And I sent an answer in a bottle back into the sea
And now I'm waiting for a reply from she

Three

Dreams

Singing
Dancing in the dew
Purple, Green, and Blue
Always spinning never stop
Waiting for the children to wake
Wild Dreams

Winter frost
It's icy cold
No more sunburns in town
Time for hot cocoa now
Earmuffs so cozy
Reindeer crossing my path

Dusk Dancers

As the sun disappears beyond the horizon
The children dance at dusk
They leap in the moonlight
Till the sun paints the streets with light
Despite what seems to be endless night

Walking in the Moonlight

She's been walking in the moonlight
Since the moonlight ever was
Starlight upon her face
She's been walking in the moonlight
When the city falls asleep
No longer hides in the shadows
Now she's been walking in the moonlight
A creature of the night

Thunder

Thunder, Thunder
Up in the clouds
Strikes you with lightning
And puts your lights out
Storm's brewing
Sky not blueing
Shades of gray
Sunshine kept at bay
Stuck inside
Spending your days away

Way Up High

Light up the night
Burn all your troubles
Follow the light
Till you banish the shadows
As a thousand colors
Streak through the sky
Way up high
Where only the moons can see
And only the stars can reach
'Cause if you only believe
You can go up there too
Just the stars and you

Love Never Leaves

Objects will get lost
Paper will rip
Memories will fade
But love never leaves
Love in you
Love in me
And I thought you knew
Love stays for eternity

Volumes

A crack in my characters
The soul of my spine
The heart of my stories
Volumes of truth and mystery
All wound up in these old pages
An epic plot answers the hero
A villain

Discover

Wander the world
Spread wisdom
Speak truth
Heal broken hearts
Imagine new beginnings
Discover life

A New Beginning

Quiver
Shake
Crack!
Look, a beak
Two little blue feet
It hatched, you see
Such a heartwarming moment
And look, a little chick sprouted
A new beginning, ready to fly
A new beginning sprouted, for you and I

Books

They taste like warm hot cocoa in a white mug
They sound like the rustle of pages
Fluttering by
They smell like crisp new papers
Or frayed old ones
They look like words, words, words
Gliding across a white background
Serene sages of ink

.

Four

If the world were made out of books

If the world were made out of books
Anyone could be what they want to be
If I was feeling sad
I would check out
A new book from the library
If I was mad at someone
We would just agree to check out
A new book from the library
If I needed to fix something
I would check out a new book at the library
So why won't anyone just
Check out a new book from the library?

Firelight

Snuggling up to the firelight
Come in, come in
It's cold outside
Huddling up in the blankets like
Two bears when it's cold outside

Tell a story
Comedic or gory
Yes, come in
Sit with me
In the rocking chair
Made of oak tree

And if you don't have just one story
Just come in and sit with me

Clouds

Cumulus, cirrus, stratus, nimbus
Twirling, playing, dancing in the sky
Born gifted shapeshifters
Gliding through the atmosphere
Sometimes we see people we've lost
Places we miss
Things we love
Millions of people can see the same cloud
But to each one of us it looks different

My Name

When I'm gone
Through dusk and dawn
I don't care
If everywhere
My name they fear
If that's all they know
In three hundred million years
I'll stay alive
In the legends
I will thrive
In the stories
They'll tell someday
I'll never go away
They'll know my name

Fiery

Smoke, Fire, Ash, Flame
A difficult fiery monster to tame
Magma, Lava, Soot, Blaze
In a fire frenzy craze
Burning
Turning
Churning
Dancing flames
Steady they rise
Flipping, running, spinning
Before our very eyes
Smoke, Fire, Ash, and Flame
Magma, Lava, Soot, Blaze

Keep Running

I want to feel the wind in my hair
Want to run as far as I dare
Want to have that feeling
When you just float off the ground
And everything is muffled in the background

Every time I touch the ground
I spring back up
Go back around
Go on, keep running
Don't stop for nothing
As I soar through the air
Wind is whipping my face
But I just don't care
And I keep running

Five

Best Friends

One is the Sun
The other the Moon
One is midnight
The other is noon
One is black
The other is white
One hangs loose
While the other is tight
One is the forest
The other is the city
One filled with arrogance
One with pity
They argue
They laugh
They love
They live
They cry
They do what they do
And they do it with pride

Angel vs Devil

Angel, Angel prancing about
Didn't know what to do
So he stopped front of Devil
Angel said
Hey I'm the better twin
I do the right thing while you sin
Devil smiled back with glee
Nah, you're wrong 'bout me
See I'm the better twin
It's all real clear
I free the forbidden
From all they fear
And what do they fear
Angel said with a pout
Devil gave a humph and sigh
Then a deep voice came out of the sky
Neither of you are the best twin
When you're really put to test
Neither of you win
Angel cried out, shaking in fear
Who are you? Are you foe or peer?
I'm the cloud, the sky, you're walking on
I'm the master, you're just a pawn
Then the cloud shifted
And dropped them into oblivion
And that's why you should never fight
Unless you're actually the better twin

Fire, Flame, Smoke, and Stars

There are people with their hearts
Set upon stone
They look up and all they see is stone
But you look up
And you see more
You see fire
You see flame
You see the smoke and the stars
You go draw outside the lines
Just to prove you could
You go break all the rules
Just to prove you would
You go beat them all
Just to prove you'll never obey
Go on and seize the day
Because you see fire
You see flame
You see the smoke and the stars
And you never forget
Why you came
And you never forget
Who you are
And you never forget
That life's more than a game
And you never forget
Your ancestors are watching
From up in the stars
Set yourself free

Traveler's Song

I've been here
I've been there
I've been practically everywhere
I make allies as I go
Catching trains, boarding boats
I'm not here
I'm not there
I am sometimes not anywhere
By the time you hear of me
I'm already gone
I have traveled by air
I have traveled by sea
Bet you haven't heard of me
This is the traveler's symphony

Still they fall

Ingots of bronze
Bullions of gold
Little shards of crimson
Flutter, flutter
Down they go
Flutter, flutter
Through the gutter
Swept away by the rain
Flooding, Flooding
Down the pipes
Up, up, high
More of them fall
Land on bright red raincoats
And black-striped umbrellas
Flutter, flutter
Still they fall
Land in your hand
Go on, take it home
And when come tomorrow
And when the sun shines
Leave it on the balcony
It needs to be dry
Open the notebook, I thought you knew
Daisies lie here and roses too
Elm and Birch scattered askew
And now one is added new

See the Light

Folks say the eyes are the windows to the soul
They say you can see someone's core
But someone's core isn't all you can see
Every eye can see hate
Every eye can see war
Every eye can see everything wrong with everyone
But green eyes
Blue eyes
Amber eyes
Hazel eyes
Brown eyes
All eyes
Can see light
But if only you look
But if only you stop seeing the darkness
And start seeing the light
Because seeing the darkness
Only creates darkness
And sometimes, you become the darkness
And when you become darkness
You cannot see the light
And if you cannot see the light
You cannot see the world
You cannot see the good
And when you look at the light
And the darkness
You see

There is more light
Than there is darkness
And here, in our world
We see darkness
We see war
We see killing
We see misinformation spread like wildfire
We cannot embrace the darkness
Welcome it in to our doorsteps
And we cannot ignore the darkness
For it will continue
So we have to change the darkness
To light.

Acknowledgements

I would like to thank my mom, who first introduced me to poetry, and my dad, who avidly read every one of my poems. I would also like to thank my other two first readers, my best friends, Julia and Hazel. All of your love and support have made this book possible. I am also grateful to Hilary Arenstein, who taught me so much about poetry and language. And, finally, I would like to thank Seth and Sapphira Edgarde at Blackbird Books for publishing this, my first poetry collection.

To see our other great titles,
visit us at:

BLACKBIRD BOOKS
www.bbirdbooks.com

Lightning Source UK Ltd.
Milton Keynes UK
UKHW010718131222
413853UK00001B/56